I0828500

For Those Who Have Made

SHIPWRECK

of Their Faith

Kent A. Philpott, MDiv, DMin

Earthen Vessel Publishing

For Those Who Have Made ShipWreck of Their Faith

Earthen Vessel Media, LLC
San Rafael, CA 94903
www.earthenvesselmedia.com.com

ISBN: 978-1-946794-37-6

Interior design by KLC Philpott

Contents

Preface

This book is written for those of you who have stumbled and fallen along the narrow way, either by means of a physical trauma, a significant loss due to death, even a moral failure including that of a sexual nature, emotional and mental collapse, and anything else that might have caused you grief and shame to the point you wanted to give it all up—or were forced to give it all up.

Somehow or another you made shipwreck of your faith. Maybe the blame is only 10% your own; maybe it is 100%—no matter. Yes, you were sealed and sanctified in the Holy Spirit upon your new birth, and your name is written in the Lamb's Book of Life, but you ended up crashing your boat against the rocks.

The Apostle John knew that genuine born-from-above Christians are yet fallen creatures. "My little children, I am writing these things to you so that you may not sin. But if anyone does sin, we have an advocate with the Father, Jesus Christ the righteous" (1 John 2:1). We are indeed a contradiction: we are both perfect in Christ and sinners at the same time. And Paul reminded us that we do not sin in order that grace may abound (see Romans 6:1). Please note that the "if" in 1 John 2:1 is, in terms of Greek grammar, the third class condition, which means a future probability; in this instance, "if" means that the apostle, and by virtual of the reality of Holy Spirit inspiration, the Triune God knew His sons and daughters would yet yield to sinful temptations.

The world, the flesh, and the devil—many have succumbed to this trinity of evil. Who has not fallen? Some of us either rebelled or were deceived, but it was caught on video for the entire world to see, or at least those in the pews played it over and over.

Now you find out how much of a minefield a church or any organization of humans can be. People, and some of these closest to you, react in ways you never anticipated, and it is not worth fixing blame. Maybe you left people no other choice, but in any case, you fell and even thought of suicide.

Being a pastor into my fifth decade, and based on what I have learned, most of our trouble has to do with sex and/or money, sometimes in combo, and when it all blows up, which it usually does, the guilt, shame, humiliation, and ensuing scandal never dies. It may be forgiven, but it is never forgotten or entirely recovered from.

Is there no hope? Must you, even if you attempt to be part of a congregation, sit in the back pew, arrive late and leave early, and conclude you have no more service to offer your Lord Jesus?

There is restoration; my life has become a testimony to that fact. Any recovery from significant loss is painful, and this book might be difficult to read, but if you will chance it, let us see where it can take you.

ONE:
For the Shipwrecked

Paul wrote an instruction to his disciple Timothy that can inspire both hope and fear:

> *This charge I entrust to you, Timothy my child, in accordance with the prophecies previous made about you, that by them you may wage the good warfare, holding faith and a good conscience. By rejecting this, some have made shipwreck of their faith, among whom are Hymenaeus and Alexander, whom I have handed over to Satan that they may learn not to blaspheme.* 1 Timothy 1:18-20

Shipwreck—does it mean the ship was sunk and that Hymenaeus and Alexander lost their salvation and are headed to hell?

Shipwreck—does it mean the boat is salvageable, but repairs must be made?

Commentators, depending on their theology, will land on one or the other interpretation. My view is that the ship needed to be hauled into dry dock and be worked on by a master ship repairer. Why else would Paul hand them over to Satan to experience what happens to a good ship when abandoned or run aground? In any case, Paul does not necessarily mean for this to be taken literally—the idea that Satan is (willingly) involved in the restoration process. The idea is that they were excommunicated or placed outside the congregation for the protection of the church but also for the purpose of restoration of the two men. Truly converted people will not want to be long out of fellowship; they will change course, rethink, and begin again.

In my case, I made shipwreck of my faith twice at least but probably more times than that. Two: that is the number of my divorces. And both while a Christian. Oh, and also while pastor of a Baptist church.

Both events are so complicated and confusing, even to this day, that I am not sure what really happened. In neither case did I want a divorce, and oddly enough, I was largely to blame for both. There is no use in going back over it all, as I do not want to seem like I am excusing myself or blaming anyone else. Divorce is sin, and I am guilty. Of course, I remarried both times, and that almost makes matters worse. There are plenty who consider that I and my current wife are living in sin.

The first one, in 1980, took place in a highly toxic environment, which was mostly caused by me alone. It took me years to recover from the loss of my first wife and more years to face up to the cultic church experience I had surrounded myself with. After I resigned from my pastorate, I was shunned and rejected along with the rest of my family, and eventually the marriage fell apart. It was horribly tragic, and the pain of it yet lingers.

The second divorce, in 2009, was tragic as well, and it was beyond my control—not to say that I was not responsible for the mess. My congregation, of which I am yet pastor, twice rejected my attempts at resigning, and these lovely and graceful people have stood with me, and together we have refused to shoot the wounded but to bind up the broken hearts.

Some of those who pastor in nearby churches do not know what to think and ignore or reject me. There are also those who know what it is like to struggle emotionally and spiritually and embrace me as a fellow traveler.

It is not easy writing these things; I do so for others who have suffered similar failures and are terribly depressed as a result. And, as the old cliché has it, the goal is to get up off the floor once you have fallen. Probably not words to live by, yet there is something valiant in the concept.

When I consider certain biblical characters, I immediately go to David and Peter, read of their total collapse, and see that their God made them stand again. Do you suppose David was a worse sinner than Peter? Many do, but consider: Peter denied Jesus three times, and was rebuked by Paul, because his "conduct was not in step with the truth of the gospel" (Galatians 2:14). Peter's error involved not only the basis of salvation but also the unity of the Church. That was a very large misstep.

The thought of having grieved a holy and loving God, according to their own writings, must have caused them considerable distress. Despite it all, they kept on following Jesus and were received back into the community of God—quite clearly so in Peter's case. Yes, there was repentance and a turning from sin, but what happened remained known to all. The people of God had learned to love one another as Jesus had loved them, and that made all the difference.

Two:
We Remain with a Fallen Nature

Paul was literally shipwrecked at least three times. The last one happened while he was being taken to Rome after he had appealed to Caesar, the Roman emperor, which was his right as a Roman citizen. The events are described in Acts 27.

The captain or pilot of the boat did not listen to Paul but sailed west from the Island of Crete out into the Adriatic Sea bound for Rome, despite the fact it was well into the stormy season. The ship, being driven by a tempestuous wind, arrived off the coast of Malta, an island south of Sicily. Hoping to enter a suitable bay, the crew did what it could, but the ship hit a hidden reef and was stuck. However, in accord with what the angel of God told Paul, all 276 hands aboard made it safely to shore.

Luke did not intend for his recounting of the tumultuous trip to Rome to be used as an analogy, but it may well serve as one. God did not abandon those on board, those who were shipwrecked, but brought them safely to shore.

Indeed, God is able to do this, even in the most extreme circumstances. Consider Romans 8:37-39:

> *No, in all these things we are more than conquerors through him who loved us. For I am sure that neither death nor life, nor angels, nor rulers, nor things present nor things to come, nor powers, nor height nor depth nor anything else in all creation, will be able to separate us from the love of God in Christ Jesus our Lord.*

Some will be quick to point out that the context of the passage is God's everlasting love, and nowhere is it mentioned that those who sin willfully in rebellious disobedience will be covered in this great and graceful love.

Somehow what concerns so many are the obvious sins, especially those that are sexual in nature. Seemingly forgotten are the lesser sins, as if there are indeed lesser sins. How anyone can read the list of the works of the flesh recorded in Galatians 6:19-21 and declare their hands are clean is almost beyond comprehension.

> *Now the works of the flesh are evident: sexual immorality, impurity, sensuality, idolatry, sorcery, enmity, strife, jealousy, fits of anger, rivalries, dissensions, divisions, envy, drunkenness, orgies, and things like these. I warn you, as I warned you before, that those who do such things will not inherit the kingdom of God.*

Let me suggest a time of prayer and reflection concerning the sins mentioned above; look into your own heart and mind, and you might find you have missed the mark on some of them. Missed the mark? How about ignored, minimized, dismissed, disregarded, or misidentified? And the sentence could get longer; yes, living is messy, and as much as we may not want to, we fall into behavior and states of mind that are other than God would want for us.

We may be tempted to excuse ourselves by pointing out that others are guilty of sin as well. We must own our personal sin and bring it to Jesus, our sin bearer, and confess our sin and ask for forgiveness. As Christians, we know this is what we do. We are the sinners who stand in the need of prayer.

Certainly, the impact or results of some sins are far more dramatic and damaging than others, but any sin is committed against a holy and righteous God. And who can stand? Only those who are clean? Let me state this strongly and directly—we are all guilty.

Paul, after listing the works of the flesh, presents the "fruit of the Spirit is love, joy, peace, patience, kindness, goodness, faithfulness, gentleness, self-control" (Galatians 6:22–23). Does anyone reading this claims that he or she exhibits such fruit on a continual basis? I have asked this of myself on a number of occasions, and never once have I been able to say that I comply.

Essentially, we are all dependent upon the power of the Holy Spirit and the grace of God. We must all rely upon the truth of passages like Hebrews 7:28: "He is able to save to the uttermost those who draw near to God through him, since he always lives to make intercession for them."

Although these great and gracious truths are plain and evident, I can still hear it as I have heard it a hundred times from well-meaning fellow Christians: "God will only forgive when a person repents and turns away from sin."

Repenting is a lifelong process. Shortly after his conversion, a friend prayed, "Lord, show me my sin." A month later he prayed, "That's enough for now." Early on, we have no idea of the depth of our own sin and the utter holiness of the Triune God, and the discovery is shocking. We see, and do agree with Scripture, that we have a fallen nature. We rejoice that the Apostle John spoke directly to our yet sinful condition and explained that we are to confess our sin to a faithful and just God who forgives our sin and cleanses us from all unrighteousness (see 1 John 1:8-2:2).

Ungracious legalism is deadening and demoralizing; it is most certainly not quickening and moralizing. The legalist is anxious that an emphasis on grace will result in cheap grace and lax morals, even libertinism. The exact opposite is true. God's graciousness draws us *toward* holiness not away from it. Those Christians who give up on themselves as totally worthless failures are heading toward a serious condition both spiritually and emotionally.

Where the balance is between self-confidence and a faithful dependence on the power of the indwelling Holy Spirit is not easily, if ever, reached. No doubt, living in the presence of God in heaven is that place. Meanwhile, we go on repenting, striving to please God and refusing to hear the damning voice of the accuser of the brethren.

One further question must be asked here: Could failures, of whatever kind, reveal there was actually no real conversion in the first place? There will be an attempt to answer this serious question in chapter seven.

THREE:
Pilgrims in a Strange Land

If you sail in uncharted waters during storms, with large rips in the sails, sharks circling the craft, and mutinies underway, the outcome can't be good. After all, you are made of clay, an earthen vessel.

There are those who apparently sail the seas unscathed. We read their biographies and marvel at their heroics, conquering for Jesus throughout their lives. Are these sanitized accounts? Is there a thing or two left out? Was their inner thought life as pure as presented? Were there not battles with the devil that were lost? Who could make the trip without incident?

The Scripture is not so eager to clean up the lives of the saints, even while accompanied by admonitions to live a godly and holy life. It is clear that holy living is not automatic. Consider again David and Peter. Then there is John Mark, whom Paul refused to take with him on the second missionary journey because of a failure on the first. But this is not about excuse-making or an invitation to hide behind the failures of others and thereby diminish or even outright deny personal culpability.

Does the devil not lurk near the door (see 1 Peter 5:8)? Does Satan not wage war against the 'woman' (see Genesis 3:15)? Do Christians not engage in spiritual warfare? If any of the foregoing statements were not true, then the biblical doctrines regarding the demonic realm would be nothing more than a hoax. While the devil may win some small skirmishes, even some battles, the final triumph goes to the Conqueror. In the meantime, by means of false signs and wonders, the lust of the flesh, the lust of the eyes, and the pride of life, the devil is a present and powerful enemy.

Should the wounded be left on the field of battle to groan and suffer? Is it right that the shipwrecked be left to fight the raging elements and the sharks in the storm-tossed seas—alone? Certainly they made their decisions; they deliberately rebelled and acted out. Shouldn't they get what they earned and deserve?

The Good News is that there is mercy and grace for the believer as well as the non-believer. The Christian, even the Christian leader, is often rejected and ignored—that is, unless he or she has a national following.

Where are the first-responders? Where are those who do not fear getting their hands soiled and even scarred? Must we really abandon those who have fallen and so avoid guilt by association? Are there those who will risk being castigated for not rejecting the beaten and robbed pilgrim?

There are such, and I have discovered them. They are brave, even fearless; they care more about the enemy not having his way with the victims, who are not without guilt, but they see a larger good, a life yet to be lived out. They care not if called "liberal" or a "partner in crime" and will risk the scorn directed at them. I have encountered a few of these good Samaritans along the journey who saw a fallen comrade battered and bloody. In their eyes they beheld a snapshot in time that told only a fraction of the story; they knew there would be more story for the telling.

FOUR:
Beginning Again

The call to love and serve the Lord is still present in those of us who crossed lines. Those called of God to serve Him in His Church will say like Paul, "Woe is me if I preach not the gospel of Christ." For the genuinely converted, this call to serve God and His Church does not vanish into thin air. However, how do we then return and start again?

BE SURE YOU HAVE RECOVERED.

This takes time and effort; it does not happen as a matter of time passing. Recovery is deliberate, not half-hearted, and it requires considerable courage. It can be a very humbling experience. Some are shocked that a Christian leader could stumble, which indicates their immaturity, having little life experience. Toleration for them is required.

BE SURE YOU HAVE REGAINED YOUR EMOTIONAL AND SPIRITUAL BALANCE.

We are likely looking at a number of years here. Indeed, you will never completely get over it. I have not; I carry my failures with me every day of my life. (Is it my thorn in the flesh?)

Perhaps even worse, there are those who actually relish reminding me of what a jerk I have been. (Is this the devil whispering in the ear? He is the accuser of the brethren, you know.)

It has come to my attention that I have harbored ill will toward those who shunned and rejected me during my crisis.

Yes, the experience has nourished bitterness in me, even anger at times, towards those who were not able to reach out to me or who even made things worse. This is on me and constitutes an area in my inner being that I must deal with in a Godly and holy manner.

DO NOT AVOID OTHERS WHO KNOW OF YOUR FAILURE.

What courage it takes to be in communication with those who know what happened to you, and even more so with those who were emotionally and/or spiritually damaged by your behavior. It may be very slow in coming.

You must even be able to face those who are rather pleased that you made a mess out of your life. And you will be surprised to find that these folks are out there and not only among the non-Christians. Some of those whom you counted as brothers and sisters in Christ will actually rejoice at your failure and adopt the attitude, "Well, I could have told you so."

At some point we will stop running away and face reality.

IDEAS ON HOW TO HELP THOSE WHO DO NOT KNOW WHAT TO DO OR SAY.

After any misfortune, we often experience how difficult it is for others to know what to say to us. "I am sorry," is about as good as most of us can do. And that is often enough.

However, there are those who will want to stand with you, even though they are troubled at what happened. You can help by direct communication and breaking the ice with a simple, non-blaming confession or statement of culpability. "Thanks for hanging with me," is a good starter statement.

Let the other person talk and, without becoming defensive, allow them to express their feelings. Bottled up emotions are painful and prevent fellowship. If you can do so, and it takes some significant recovery, let a person say what they will and without the need to defend, excuse, or explain. Confession works in many different ways, and it is good for us to do and to hear it.

GUARD YOURSELF FROM MAKING THE SAME MISTAKES AGAIN.

There will more on this in the next chapter, but we must admit to ourselves that we are vulnerable to making the very same mistakes again. Patterns of behavior are learned when we are young and usually stick with us. Even if we have an insight into our own behavior, it may not be enough to avoid going that way again. The word is accountability, especially when you realize the flesh is weak, and having a relationship with someone where there is genuine accountability is a rare thing. I must warn that care must be exercised here, since it is not uncommon for those in whom we confide to later betray us.

FORGIVE THOSE WHO HAVE REJECTED YOU.

As followers of Jesus we are called to forgive those who spitefully use and abuse us. We may, in our pain and suffering, think that we are the ones to be sought after and confession made to. This cannot be presumed, however, and it may never take place, but it is our responsibility to fulfill the law of Christ to love one another. A large part of this is to forgive those who have hurt us. Jesus took it to the point, as you well know, of admonishing that we love our enemies, not oppose them or even just tolerate them.

DON'T GO WHERE YOU ARE NOT WANTED.

Look for a spiritual community to be part of and to which you can be accountable, one that is Christ-centered and Bible-believing. (You might be surprised what you will find.) However, avoid going to gatherings or places where you are not wanted or where your presence may cause difficulty.

I have known pastors who served congregations for many years with blood, sweat, and tears, and desired to continue the relationships therein. While continuing relationships may exist, it may not be the responsible thing to do to intrude yourself in a situation where you are not wanted. Indeed, there will be situations where you are not wanted, and you will know when these arise. It is best to let things be, though it may be excruciatingly painful.

Start small, and in the next chapter I will go into this in greater detail.

FIVE:
Rebuilding and Restoring

Now, first of all, the wrecked ship needs restoring and repairing. The damaged hulk will have to be dragged off the rocks and hauled to a safe place for rebuilding and restoring. No such place may be available, which is not unusual. There are generally few resources to cover the costs of the time and money involved. There is often absolutely no help at all.

Christian leaders may actually want to be out from underneath the pressures that go with ministry. They may create a crisis, even on an subconscious level, which effectively forces an end to a ministry. This, in fact, describes many leadership failures. In such circumstances, the minister may eventually, after rebuilding, long to be back in action—somehow, somewhere.

Most people do not realize the pressures weighing on a minister, especially on the pastor of a congregation. The pastor/teacher is carrying a load that few are aware of. Pastors rarely feel as though they are succeeding and are mostly aware of what is not getting done. They are painfully acquainted with people who are hurting and whom they do not seem to be able to help and encourage. Other care-giving professionals rely on creating distance from those they serve, but this does not work in Christian ministry. The load is upon the shoulders, and it never lets up. How many pastors actually commit suicide is unknown, but from what I have gathered, it is nevertheless a small but quantifiable percentage. It is then obvious the size of the rebuilding job that may be necessary.

There are many ways to serve our Lord Jesus other than pastoring a church. Though the church is a vital venue for service, it is not the only one. It may be publishing, writing, evangelism, serving abroad in difficult places; it may be as simple as handing bulletins to worshipers on Sunday morning. Over the years, I have found a number of those who were drummed out of the professional ministry, and some of them for good reason, who created businesses of one kind or another and therein found ways to count and witness. Whatever it may be, there will be a place to work for the Kingdom. The manager of the vineyard will find work for any who want it, even for those who show up late.

Our concern here now is rebuilding and restoration. I have learned that healing from a catastrophic collapse is not simply accomplished. Perhaps it will be a lonely and private struggle, as some Christian communities practice effective shunning techniques. Or, due to circumstances, there may be no time or money for such.

Ministers who must suddenly leave their place of employment are often without resources. What then? Here is where the internet might be helpful. If drugs or alcohol are involved, there are Twelve Step programs, which can be wonderful. These folks know what it is to stumble and to do so badly. They will be welcoming and affirming. Within the broad range of groups within the Twelve Step family are also groups that involve issues other than substance abuse. And there are men's groups of all sorts. Some of these can be discovered on MeetUp.com.

There are Christian congregations that have mature believers who can be counted on, even among churches that are Christ-centered and biblically faithful. Christianity is far from a cookie-cutter phenomenon. It takes searching, asking, phoning, whatever it takes—but the point is, no one can do it alone. Even those who take up a monkish lifestyle and head for the desert or a mountain to pray, meditate, reflect, repent, and go back to basics—this is only a beginning. The Church, the blood-bought community of faith, that gathering where Jesus walks in its midst, is the place of ultimate healing.

After a crisis, some Christian leaders fall apart and apparently, seemingly, depart from the faith. I have seen plenty of this. I have also seen that some of these "fallen" often make a comeback at some point. This is more often the case than one of no return. Once born again from above and one is a son or daughter of God, this does not change. Parents know that whatever happens, their kids are still their kids. Is it not so with the Father—does He not continue to love His erring and damaged children? Will He not lead them out of sin and its consequences and into green pastures? You know the answer, at least in your head if not in your heart.

Let us examine, briefly, some helpful passages of Scripture that speak to our issue.

James 5:19–20 reads:

> *[19] My brothers, if anyone among you wanders from the truth and someone brings him back, [20] let him know that whoever brings back a sinner from his wandering will save his soul from death and will cover a multitude of sins.*

James, half-brother of Jesus, who many think was the first pastor of the first Christian congregation in Jerusalem, whose letter is likely the very first inspired document to emerge from the Christian Church, speaks to the issue of shipwreck very directly. The "if" in the first sentence is a conditional clause of the third class and is predicting the high probability of an event where someone wanders from the truth. To wander or stray from the truth is certainly a shipwreck scenario. Pastor James was concerned about such brothers and sisters and encourages members of the flock to bring them back, the result of which is of the highest good.

James does not consider these wandering sheep as hopelessly lost at all. Perhaps echoing the teaching of the Good Shepherd who leaves the ninety-nine and goes out searching for the single lost lamb, he actually concludes his general pastoral letter with this beautiful, sensitive, and realistic admonition.

In 1 Timothy 3:1–13, we find Paul's qualifications for overseers and deacons. The lists are formidable indeed: above reproach, the husband of one wife, sober-minded, self-controlled, respectable, hospitable, able to teach, not a drunkard, not violent but gentle, not quarrelsome, not a lover of money, a good manager of his household, have submissive children, not a recent convert, well thought of by non-Christians, dignified, not double-tongued, not addicted to much wine, not greedy, having a thorough understanding of the Faith, tested beforehand so as to prove themselves blameless, and with wives who are dignified, not slanderers, sober-minded, and faithful in all things.

It might also be helpful to look at 1 Thessalonians 4:1–12 as well.

My thinking is that if anyone of us in Christian leadership was to sober-mindedly examine these qualifications, we would have to resign immediately. The calling is extraordinarily high, and this is in addition to loving the Lord our God with all we are and our neighbor as ourselves!

As I write this section, I cannot help but say to myself, "Woe is me! For I am lost; for I am a man of unclean lips, and I dwell in the midst of a people of unclean lips; for my eyes have seen the King, the LORD of hosts!" (Isaiah 6:5) Then the angel of God assured Isaiah, to whom the words were directed, that by the grace and mercy of God he was forgiven and by that grace he would fulfill his calling.

By my own strength I can only fail. Though appearing outwardly like I am faithful and obedient, I would know, and I do know, that I do not measure up. Though I may often be briefly commendable, to be honest, I do not qualify. The issue is that no one does, and those who do not know this about themselves are like a mine in the minefield. Am I too harsh in my judgment after fifty-two years in pastoral ministry? I think not.

SIX:
What Ministry or Outreach Now?

Though I have hinted at possibilities before, let's take it a little further.

There has been a time or two when people acquainted with my failures/struggles have shown up at the church I pastor to see if there may not be hope for them also. They feel secure with the thought they will not be rejected or ignored. In the most recent event of this nature the person did not announce himself, describe his situation, whine, blame, or complain but simply got involved a little at a time. In time we talked, and I found out all I needed to know.

That last sentence is somewhat important. I do not need to know the details, and I do not ask for them. If the details emerge, all right, but it is not necessary. I find it helpful to avoid my natural curiosity or prurient interest in how or "who done it." Yes, I am concerned to protect the congregation from anything of a predatory nature, and if information is revealed in the person's past history, then I want to discuss this but in a manner that is not a deal breaker for the person's recovery.

Let me simply say that I have likely heard it all, or close to it. A reader might suppose I am looking for sexual stuff, affairs, homosexuality, child molestation, rape, and so on. And these are indeed serious and must be dealt with at some point before any kind of ministry opens up. I heard someone say decades ago, "Truth is communicated across a bridge of love." This form of love, this agape love, is what Paul is talking about in 1 Corinthians 13. It, as the old Jesus People chorus has it, is to "save each one's dignity and save each one's pride."

Dignity can be so thoroughly trashed that chronic depression sets in and never or nearly ever goes away. Dignity is that sense of ourselves that we are loved by God and, though erring, are yet in the Family of God and cherished. Pride, not the selfish sort of thing where we think more highly of ourselves than we ought, but that sense of ourselves as worthy in Christ and not in ourselves, is where we can go. Dignity and pride: these are both worth preserving and building upon, as they are crucial elements in recovery from serious failure.

Now then, some thoughts on how to go about taking the risk of serving the Lord once again in an active and public manner despite failure. First of all, this is approached a little at a time, taking baby steps, rebuilding confidence slowly over a period of time.

In the context of an actual congregation, I find that the choir is great for this, maybe a praise band, or something akin. Ushering, perhaps clean-up, set-up, take-down, practical things that are relatively safe to do. By safe I mean that there are fewer chances for criticism due to inconsistency, absence, or getting things confused. With support and instruction, a former preacher/teacher can be re-introduced to these, but here the possibility for a failure grows exponentially. When one stands before the congregation as a worship leader, Scripture reader, Bible teacher, or Gospel preacher, much more is expected or even demanded. Here now is when the mentor, even if considerably younger than the mentee, plays a large role but one I cannot spell out here.

Outside a congregational setting the possibilities are many and varied. There is blogging, podcasting, and various social media platforms to utilize, but these do not provide the person-to-person contact that many hope for. That aside, it may be a place to start. In the community there are hospitals, hospices, retirement communities, and a myriad of other volunteer opportunities. There are para-church ministries, rescue missions, evangelistic outreaches, prison ministries, and the list goes on. Internet searches can open up a world unknown.

Let me re-emphasize: before we start anew, we must be careful that we have recovered sufficiently to trust ourselves and not betray the trust of others. Here we must be honest with ourselves. And there should obviously be at least one other person who knows who we are and to whom we can be accountable.

SEVEN:
Is False Conversion a Possibility?

That people are falsely converted to Christ has been observed throughout the Church's history. Every pastor, at least those who have been in place a decade or so, are well aware of false conversions. Perhaps this is a time for those of us who have not lived up to the high calling of service in the church, particularly for one of the offices in the Church (see Ephesians 4:11-13), to examine our conversion. Paul spoke of a spiritual self examination in 2 Corinthians 13:5:

> *Examine yourselves to see whether you are in the faith; test yourselves. Do you not realize that Christ Jesus is in you, unless, of course, you fail the test?*

This is not to say that a false conversion must have occurred if there has been a failure, of whatever nature. Some whom I considered the morally finest Christians I have ever met, turned out to be or proved to be unconverted people. Moral uprightness is good but not proof of genuine salvation. Were not the religious leaders of Jesus' day at least outwardly holy? And it is likely that these priests, synagogue leaders, scribes, and so on, were rarely if ever found out. And no one of us has ever been completely found out; this will only happen on the Day of Judgment at the end of the age.

Maybe I should not write what follows, but I have discovered over the decades of my ministry that only those who have been born from above will risk the kind of examination Paul urges to the Corinthians. It is generally known among pastors that only the regenerate are concerned about their salvation, since they know that this is the only real issue in all of life. There are likely exceptions to this rule, but most pastoral veterans will say the same.

WHAT CAN THE UNCONVERTED DO?

What about false conversion? I am aware that false conversions do occur, as any pastor will observe and most Christians also realize.

There is a bit of a paradox involved here. On one hand, we must be called and elected, and at the same time, we must trust Jesus as our Savior and Lord. The paradox is that, on the one hand we are called to believe in Jesus, and yet God will save those whom He has elected or chosen. Yes, there is the Arminian position and the Calvinistic position, and I embrace both at once. This is the paradox—two truths alongside each other like train tracks.

There is more that could be said here, but I want to move on to a brief examination of at least some means that may result in false conversions. These are: decisional conversion; doctrinal conversion, generational or cultural conversion; moralistic conversion; imitative conversion, and experience-based conversion.

MEANS OF FALSE CONVERSION

DECISIONAL CONVERSION

It is highly likely that Charles G. Finney, between the years 1825 and 1840, developed ways in which a person could supposedly become a Christian. He invited seekers forward to occupy the "anxious seat" and to eventually recite a prayer that was essentially a decision to invite Christ to be one's Savior and Lord. It proved to be a useful tool, and it spread and spread and spread, unto the present day. Make the decision, pray the prayer, and shazzam, you were saved. It happened to me as well, and for nearly three decades I was a Finney man.

Later on, I learned that this was tantamount to forcing God's hand, at best, and even magical thinking or practice, at worst. God, in this scenario, is not sovereign and in control; no, the one who would or would not pray the prayer is in charge.

Could it be that someone, maybe aged eight or eighty, prayed the prayer, and then it was confirmed by someone that this person was now born again? A conversion was announced, and all on the basis of someone following instructions to pray a prayer.

In my experience as a Gospel preacher, to be as honest as I can, it seems to me that sometimes the prayer resulted in a genuine salvation experience, and other times, at some point further on, it was clear that there had not been a real experience of salvation.

Doctrinal Conversion

Believing rightly or correctly, answering the catechetical questions properly—does this mean that one is certainly a Christian? I have made this error any number of times. Upon finding a fellow traveler who had all the right statements of doctrine, surely this meant I was in the company of a true Christian brother or sister.

While it is fine to think biblically and be theologically solid, this does not equate with true conversion. This error may be even more prevalent than decisional conversion, even among fundamentalists and evangelicals.

Generational or Cultural Conversion

If I live in America, I am Christian. I was not living in a Hindu, Buddhist, or Muslim nation, so I counted myself a Christian. When I enlisted in the military in 1961, I checked that I was a Protestant of the Episcopal variety. This last designation was based on the pop, sociologically-oriented book *The Status Seekers,* where I learned Episcopalians were the most prestigious and of the highest socio-economic level.

I was obviously a Christian, because I was born and raised in the good U S of A, and if everyone I knew did not count themselves Christian, at least the founding fathers had been, and Christianity permeated the culture.

One of my parents was a Christian, my grandparents had been, and I must be, too. That did it for me.

MORALISTIC CONVERSION

It seems as though I was quite moral up until the age of fifteen when things went south. Lust set in, the never-ending weird thoughts going through the brain at 100 mph; I was doomed, is how I put it. Other vices set in as well. There was no hope for me, and I knew it, so I did not try to hide behind the idea I was morally upright. Thank goodness.

There is a twist to this, however. What I discovered, and I found this within myself, was that after my conversion, my genuine conversion, I fell into the idea that I was now morally upright, and I noticed more than ever before that others were not. All the sins, except for a few, that the good Baptist pastor of mine spoke of I had pretty much stopped, at least for fairly long stretches at a time. Of course, I found interesting ways to justify periodic lapses.

Over the years I have found many who pride themselves on not only their doctrinal correctness but that they succeeded in leaving the unclean world and had devoted themselves to Christ. In thought and action, all was well.

The two in combination are a deadly concoction, one that lulls one to sleep before the brain function closes down completely. The fact is, there is nothing a person can do in terms of "work" that can affect salvation. Nothing at all; this is the plain biblical truth.

CONVERSION BY IMITATION

During the 1970s I pastored an evangelical church that was

fairly charismatic. As the years progressed, I came to think that if a person moved and swayed to the music, closed one's eyes, raised the arms to heaven, and shouted out a few hallelujahs, then salvation must be in place. And wow, if one spoke in tongues, that sealed it. The trouble that resulted is something I may never get over.

What can be seen and heard can be imitated. To be part of the group, to be in, to win acceptance, even status, only required imitating the behavior of existing group members, which is not very difficult. I have known preachers who wowed the crowd and even had spiritual gifts, especially that of healing, who were about as converted as a demon. And this last sentence I do not write easily.

EXPERIENCE BASED CONVERSION

To have what is thought to be an "experience with God," which is widely promoted these days, is to assume that one must be born again. How about "lying under the power of God" on the floor, maybe for hours, even days—does this not assure that one is a child of God? Hmmm, I fail to think of a verse or two that supports this.

If one is healed, does this prove one is also then born again? Again, in vain do I look for a verse that supports such a notion. Witnessing a miracle or being present when one is told the Holy Spirit is moving in power—these can be false signs and wonders. It is abundantly clear that Satan performs his miracles, and like a famous baseball broadcaster once said, "Look it up."

Nowhere in Scripture, and I mean nowhere, is there any idea expressed that we are to seek after an "experience" with God. The counterfeit for a simple trusting in Jesus Christ as Savior and Lord is experience, perhaps in an altered state of consciousness where anything might be experienced and none of which is good. This is no proof of anything at all. Salvation is not a feeling or an experience.

CAN ANYONE EVER BE SURE?

Some say yes, some say no to this question. There is Romans 8:16: "The Spirit himself bears witness with our spirit that we are children of God,..." The Holy Spirit convinces us, but this is internal and individual, undocumented, and mysterious.

There are the traditional "marks" of a Christian: conviction of sin, revelation of Jesus as Savior and Lord, belief in the truth of the crucifixion and resurrection, moral change, love of God, worship of God, desire to know Jesus more, fellowship with other Christians, desire for baptism, love of receiving the bread and the cup, faithfulness to serve, worship with tithes and offerings, continuing desire to turn from sin, ongoing repentance, enduring the race, and getting back up if one should fall.

When I look at myself, I see many of the marks of a Christian. It does seem to me that the Spirit of God indwells me and convinces me that I really am in the Family of God. Yet these are inner convictions, subjective not objective; thus there is room for doubt.

What to do? Follow Jesus in faithful service and worship in any case. If I became convinced that I was not among the elect, never mind, I would continue anyway. And this alone proves nothing except that at minimum you recognize following the truth of Scripture results in a more meaningful and better life than the converse.

Some of the Puritans would say that whether they are converted or not is something they will leave in the hands of God. For them, they would faithfully follow Jesus as Lord in any case. Perhaps they were guarding against pride or presumption, but they did not rely on a sense of assurance. Assurance is blessed indeed, but even here it is not essential.

For more thoughts on the subject of conversion, please read my book, *A Matter of Life and Death*, also previously published with the title, *Are You Really Born Again?*

EIGHT:
Be Part of the Story

This brief note is for those who would like to contribute your story for a future edition.

What I have learned and experienced I have passed on to you. You may now like to do the same for others.

I invite you to send me your story. Since I will not be able to re-write or edit much of anything, please go over every sentence carefully. What you send in is what will be published in a future edition. As you write, have in mind that person out there who is so depressed and discouraged that they are not sure they can carry on.

My email is: kentphilpott@comcast.net.

May God richly bless you!

www.ingramcontent.com/pod-product-compliance
Lightning Source LLC
LaVergne TN
LVHW052343100826
845147LV00021B/1171

* 9 7 8 1 9 4 6 7 9 4 3 7 6 *